P9-DHA-910

CURRICULUM LIBRARY

Mysterious Thelonious

Chris Raschka
VI·10·98

Chris Raschka

ORCHARD BOOKS   NEW YORK

Copyright © 1997 by Christopher Raschka
All rights reserved. No part of this book may be reproduced or
transmitted in any form or by any means, electronic or mechanical,
including photocopying, recording, or by any information storage or
retrieval system, without permission in writing from the Publisher.

Orchard Books, 95 Madison Avenue, New York, NY 10016

Manufactured in the United States of America
Printed by Barton Press, Inc.
Bound by Horowitz/Rae
The text of this book is hand lettered.
The illustrations are watercolor
reproduced in full color.

Library of Congress Cataloging-in-Publication Data
Raschka, Christopher.
Mysterious Thelonious / Chris Raschka.   p.   cm.
Summary: Matches the tones of the chromatic scale
to the values of the color wheel in presenting a
portrait of the work of the Afro-American jazz
musician and composer of "Misterioso."
ISBN 0-531-30057-9   ISBN 0-531-33057-5 (lib. bdg.)
1. Monk, Thelonious—Pictorial works—Juvenile
literature. [1. Monk, Thelonious. 2. Musicians.
3. Jazz. 4. Afro-Americans—Biography.] I. Title.
ML3930.M66R37 1997
786.2'165'092—dc21   97-6994

10 9 8 7 6 5 4 3 2 1

CURR
ML

3930
.M66
R37
1997
C.2

for Dick Jackson

stor-

is

a

This

Monk

ni-

Jus

lo-

his sic. and mu-

no

no

had

a-

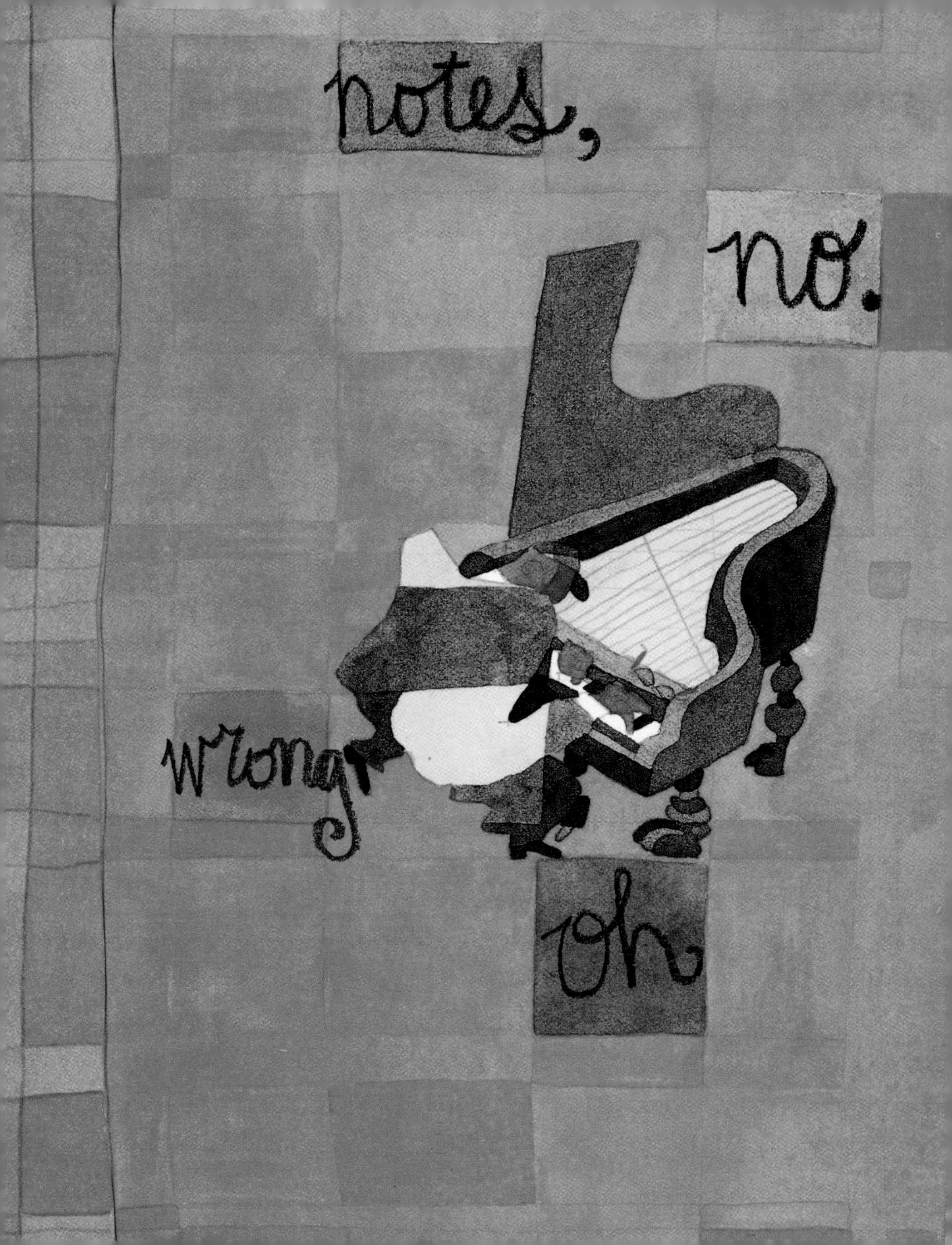
notes,
no.
wrong
oh

stor-

is

a

This

sic

ly

mu-

love-

one

played

not

He

note,

one.

wrong,

not

none, one.

had not

mu-

played

the

He

is   pic-

a

This

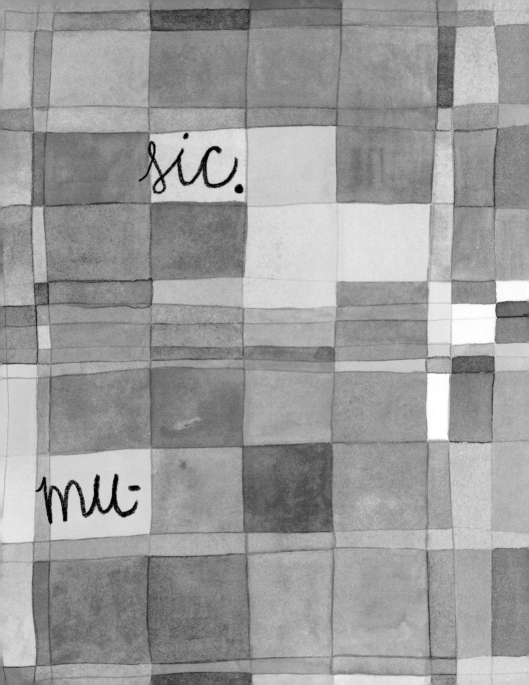

ous

ter-   lo-

ous,

i-

mys-   The-

ni-

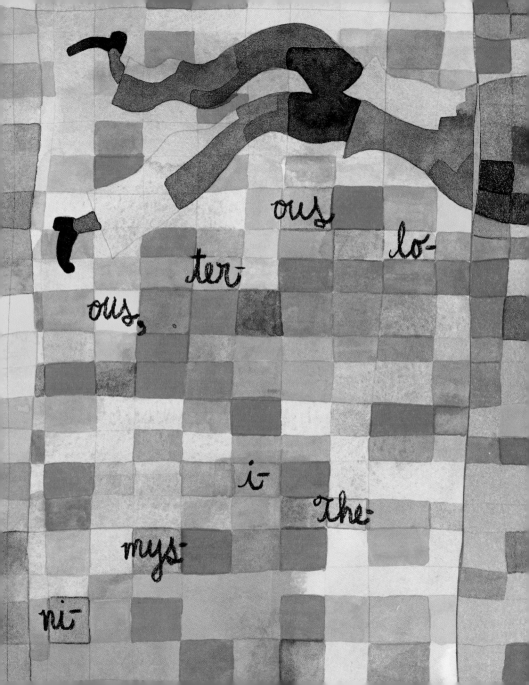

"WITHDRAWN"
LIBRARY COLLEGE LIBRARY

"WITHDRAWN"
JUNIATA COLLEGE LIBRARY

CURRICULUM LIBRARY